This Book
Belongs To:

_____

LIBRARY *of* CLASSIC POETS

Carl Sandburg

Selected Poems

Elizabeth Barrett Browning: Selected Poems

Emily Dickinson: Selected Poems

Robert Frost: Selected Poems

Henry Wadsworth Longfellow: Selected Poems

Edgar Allan Poe: Complete Poems

Carl Sandburg: Selected Poems

Walt Whitman: Selected Poems

William Butler Yeats: Selected Poems

Carl Sandburg

Selected Poems

Gramercy Books
New York

This 2004 edition is published by Gramercy Books, an imprint of Random
House Value Publishing, a division of Random House, Inc., New York.

Gramercy is a registered trademark and the colophon
is a trademark of Random House, Inc.

Random House
New York • Toronto • London • Sydney • Auckland
www.randomhouse.com

Printed and bound in the United States of America

This work was originally published by Random House Value Publishing
in March 2001 in another format.

ISBN: 0-517-21510-1

Special Edition
9 8 7 6 5 4 3 2 1

CONTENTS

Handfuls

War Poems
(1914–1915)

The Road and the End

Fogs and Fires

Shadows

Other Days
(1900–1910)

In Reckless Ecstasy

INTRODUCTION

Carl Sandburg (1878–1967) won the Pulitzer Prize twice, first for his biography of Abraham Lincoln in 1940 and then for his collected poems in 1951. And while these two prizes sum up the main themes of his life's work, the award he valued most, the one he kept where he could look at it every day, was the award he received in 1965: a Life Membership in the National Association for the Advancement of Colored People. Roy Wilkins called him "a major prophet of Civil Rights in our time"—a suitable honor for the quintessential poet of the people.

Sandburg was the son of Swedish immigrants who had moved to Galesburg, Illinois, to escape a life of poverty in Europe. His father, August, worked for the Chicago, Burlington and Quincy Railroad ten hours a day, six days a week, for thirty-five years. Even so, Carl had to leave school after eighth grade, to help support the family during the hard times following the Panic of 1893. He delivered newspapers, swept floors, became a porter in a barbershop and a farmhand on a dairy farm—and all the while dreamed of the world beyond Galesburg.

When he was eighteen, and his father gave him a railroad pass (to which August was entitled as an employee), Carl made his first trip—to Chicago. This was the beginning of a life of almost continual travel. Soon afterward, in 1897, when the fortunes of the family began to improve, Carl set out for the wheatfields of Kansas, in search of the adventure of the open road.

After a year of traveling, doing odd jobs to support himself, Sandburg served in the Spanish American War. This was a turning point for him: As a veteran he could attend Lombard College in Galesburg tuition free. (He had to take some courses in the college's preparatory school, to make up for his lack of a high school education.)

At Lombard, Sandburg distinguished himself as an orator and as an editor for the school newspaper and the yearbook. He played football, and he began to write poetry. He joined the Poor Writer's Club, an informal literary society sponsored by Professor Philip Green Wright. (Wright published Sandburg's first book of poems, *In Reckless Ecstasy*, in 1904.)

But he was restless. At twenty-four, with two years left to attain his degree, Sandburg decided it was time to move on. Writing poetry and supporting himself by selling stereoscopic photographs and viewers door-to-door, Sandburg moved from town to town through the Midwest. He considered a career as an orator—he had been a successful speaker in college—and in those days, people flocked to hear lecturers speak on topics ranging from religion and politics to science and literature. He worked up a lecture on Walt Whitman, a poet who had influenced his own work, and tried to get bookings.

At the same time, his working-class background and liberal views made him sympathetic to the goals of the socialist movement in Wisconsin. He began to write articles and editorials for the party newspaper, and soon he was working for the Social-Democrats as an organizer. His efforts helped elect Emil Seidel, the first socialist mayor of Milwaukee. Seidel made Sandburg his private secretary after the election.

In 1908 Sandburg married a fellow socialist, Lilian Steichen (sister of the photographer, Edward Steichen), whom he called Paula. Margaret, the first of their three daughters, was born three years later, and the Sandburgs needed more money. Carl's tireless work for the party was satisfying, but it did not pay well. In 1912, they moved to Chicago, where Carl worked for several newspapers. Finally, he joined the *Chicago Daily News,* where he stayed for twelve years.

During his years in politics, Sandburg wrote poetry only in spare moments and primarily because Paula urged him to. It was she who submitted what he wrote to magazines. Her belief in his gifts was not shaken by the repeated rejection slips.

Then, in 1914, *Poetry,* at that time a new periodical, accepted a group of Sandburg's poems called "Chicago Poems." The magazine was beginning to make a name for itself by publishing experimental modern verse by such poets as William Butler Yeats, Ezra Pound, Amy Lowell, and Robert Frost. Sandburg's work was in good company.

The city of Chicago had had a galvanizing effect on Sandburg's work: a comparison of the poems in his first collection and those in "Chicago Poems" reveals the development of a style uniquely his own, with an innovative approach to free verse stripped of allusion and traditional poetic devices. Chicago and the everyday life of its people (from ditchdiggers to prostitutes) was his subject matter, which he treated as realistically as he saw it. He said, "Here is the difference between Dante, Milton, and me. They wrote about hell and never saw the place. I wrote about Chicago after looking the town over for years and years."

His vigorous colloquial language—a vocabulary that fits what it describes—shocked readers accustomed to finding elegance and grace in poetry. Many were outraged by his use of slang and earthy idiom—and some critics argued that what he wrote was not poetry at all.

But Theodore Dreiser, the great modern American social novelist, said Sandburg had "the ability to choose the precise word and put it in the right place, though the word might be vulgar in the eyes of the traditionalists." Time has proved Dreiser right.

Chicago Poems (most of which appears in this anthology) marked Sandburg's emergence both as a major poet and the voice of the American working class. His second book, it was published in 1916 and includes the groundbreaking poems published in *Poetry*. It was followed by five more books of poetry, which were gathered together in 1951—a collection for which Sandburg won the Pulitzer Prize.

Sandburg was also a respected historian, and his six-volume biography of Abraham Lincoln reflected his deep interest in the greatest American hero of the nineteenth century.

For this son of hard-working immigrants, the United States was the Promised Land—and his is the voice of the national bard.

CHRISTOPHER MOORE

New York
1992

Chicago
Poems

CHICAGO

Hog Butcher for the World,
Tool Maker, Stacker of Wheat,
Player with Railroads and the Nation's Freight
  Handler;
Stormy, husky, brawling,
City of the Big Shoulders:

They tell me you are wicked and I believe them, for I
  have seen your painted women under the gas lamps
  luring the farm boys.
And they tell me you are crooked and I answer: Yes, it is
  true I have seen the gunman kill and go free to kill
  again.
And they tell me you are brutal and my reply is: On the
  faces of women and children I have seen the marks
  of wanton hunger.
And having answered so I turn once more to those who
  sneer at this my city, and I give them back the sneer
  and say to them:
Come and show me another city with lifted head singing
  so proud to be alive and coarse and strong and cunning.
Flinging magnetic curses amid the toil of piling job on
  job, here is a tall bold slugger set vivid against the
  little soft cities;
Fierce as a dog with tongue lapping for action, cunning
  as a savage pitted against the wilderness,
    Bareheaded,
    Shoveling,
    Wrecking,
    Planning,
    Building, breaking, rebuilding,

Under the smoke, dust all over his mouth, laughing with
white teeth,
Under the terrible burden of destiny laughing as a young
man laughs,
Laughing even as an ignorant fighter laughs who has
never lost a battle,
Bragging and laughing that under his wrist is the pulse,
and under his ribs the heart of the people,
Laughing!
Laughing the stormy, husky, brawling laughter of Youth,
half-naked, sweating, proud to be Hog Butcher,
Tool Maker, Stacker of Wheat, Player with Railroads and Freight Handler to the Nation.

SKETCH

The shadows of the ships
Rock on the crest
In the low blue luster
Of the tardy and the soft inrolling tide.

A long brown bar at the dip of the sky
Puts an arm of sand in the span of salt.

The lucid and endless wrinkles
Draw in, lapse and withdraw.
Wavelets crumble and white spent bubbles
Wash on the floor of the beach.

      Rocking on the crest
      In the low blue luster
      Are the shadows of the ships.

MASSES

Among the mountains I wandered and saw blue haze and
    red crag and was amazed:
On the beach where the long push under the endless tide
    maneuvers, I stood silent;
Under the stars on the prairie watching the Dipper slant
    over the horizon's grass, I was full of thoughts.
Great men, pageants of war and labor, soldiers and work-
    ers, mothers lifting their children—these all I
    touched, and felt the solemn thrill of them.
And then one day I got a true look at the Poor, millions
    of the Poor, patient and toiling; more patient than
    crags, tides, and stars; innumerable, patient as the
    darkness of night—and all broken, humble ruins of
    nations.

LOST

Desolate and lone
All night long on the lake
Where fog trails and mist creeps,
The whistle of a boat
Calls and cries unendingly,
Like some lost child
In tears and trouble
Hunting the harbor's breast
And the harbor's eyes.

THE HARBOR

Passing through huddled and ugly walls
By doorways where women
Looked from their hunger-deep eyes,
Haunted with shadows of hunger-hands,
Out from the huddled and ugly walls,
I came sudden, at the city's edge,
On a blue burst of lake,
Long lake waves breaking under the sun
On a spray-flung curve of shore;
And a fluttering storm of gulls,
Masses of great gray wings
And flying white bellies
Veering and wheeling free in the open.

THEY WILL SAY

Of my city the worst that men will ever say is this:
You took little children away from the sun and the
     dew,
And the glimmers that played in the grass under the
     great sky,
And the reckless rain; you put them between walls
To work, broken and smothered, for bread and wages,
To eat dust in their throats and die empty-hearted
For a little handful of pay on a few Saturday nights.

MILL DOORS

You never come back.
I say good-by when I see you going in the doors,
The hopeless open doors that call and wait
And take you then for—how many cents a day?
How many cents for the sleepy eyes and fingers?

I say good-by because I know they tap your wrists,
In the dark, in the silence, day by day,
And all the blood of you drop by drop,
And you are old before you are young.
You never come back.

HALSTED STREET CAR

Come you, cartoonists,
Hang on a strap with me here
At seven o'clock in the morning
On a Halsted street car.

Take your pencils
And draw these faces.

Try with your pencils for these crooked faces,
That pig-sticker in one corner—his mouth—
That overall factory girl—her loose cheeks.

Find for your pencils
A way to mark your memory
Of tired empty faces.

After their night's sleep,
In the moist dawn
And cool daybreak,
    Faces
Tired of wishes,
Empty of dreams.

CLARK STREET BRIDGE

Dust of the feet
And dust of the wheels,
Wagons and people going,
All day feet and wheels.

Now.   .   .
.   .   Only stars and mist
A lonely policeman,
Two cabaret dancers,
Stars and mist again,
No more feet or wheels,
No more dust and wagons.

Voices of dollars
And drops of blood
.   .   .   .   .
Voices of broken hearts,
.   .   Voices singing, singing,
.   .   Silver voices, singing,
Softer than the stars,
Softer than the mist.

PASSERS-BY

Passers-by,
Out of your many faces
Flash memories to me
Now at the day end
Away from the sidewalks
Where your shoe soles traveled
And your voices rose and blent
To form the city's afternoon roar
Hindering an old silence.

Passers-by,
I remember lean ones among you,
Throats in the clutch of a hope,
Lips written over with strivings,
Mouths that kiss only for love,
Records of great wishes slept with,
    Held long
And prayed and toiled for:

    Yes,
Written on
Your mouths
And your throats
I read them
When you passed by.

THE WALKING MAN OF RODIN

Legs hold a torso away from the earth.
And a regular high poem of legs is here.
Powers of bone and cord raise a belly and lungs
Out of ooze and over the loam where eyes look and ears
    hear
And arms have a chance to hammer and shoot and run
    motors.
        You make us
        Proud of our legs, old man.

And you left off the head here,
The skull found always crumbling neighbor of the
    ankles.

SUBWAY

Down between the walls of shadow
Where the iron laws insist,
  The hunger voices mock.

The worn wayfaring men
With the hunched and humble shoulders,
  Throw their laughter into toil.

THE SHOVEL MAN

On the street
Slung on his shoulder is a handle half way across,
Tied in a big knot on the scoop of cast iron
Are the overalls faded from sun and rain in the ditches;
Spatter of dry clay sticking yellow on his left sleeve
    And a flimsy shirt open at the throat,
    I know him for a shovel man,
    A dago working for a dollar six bits a day
And a dark-eyed woman in the old country dreams of him
    for one of the world's ready men with a pair of fresh
    lips and a kiss better than all the wild grapes that
    ever grew in Tuscany.

A TEAMSTER'S FAREWELL

Sobs En Route to a Penitentiary

Good-by now to the streets and the clash of wheels and
    locking hubs,
The sun coming on the brass buckles and harness knobs,
The muscles of the horses sliding under their heavy
    haunches,
Good-by now to the traffic policeman and his whistle,
The smash of the iron hoof on the stones,
All the crazy wonderful slamming roar of the street—
O God, there's noises I'm going to be hungry for.

FISH CRIER

I know a Jew fish crier down on Maxwell Street with a
    voice like a north wind blowing over corn stubble in
    January.
He dangles herring before prospective customers evinc-
    ing a joy identical with that of Pavlowa dancing.
His face is that of a man terribly glad to be selling fish,
    terribly glad that God made fish, and customers to
    whom he may call his wares from a pushcart.

PICNIC BOAT

Sunday night and the park policemen tell each other it is
    dark as a stack of black cats on Lake Michigan.
A big picnic boat comes home to Chicago from the peach
    farms of Saugatuck.
Hundreds of electric bulbs break the night's darkness, a
    flock of red and yellow birds with wings at a stand-
    still.
Running along the deck railings are festoons and leaping
    in curves are loops of light from prow and stern to
    the tall smokestacks.
Over the hoarse crunch of waves at my pier comes a
    hoarse answer in the rhythmic oompa of the brasses
    playing a Polish folk song for the homecomers.

HAPPINESS

I asked professors who teach the meaning of life to tell
   me what is happiness.
And I went to famous executives who boss the work of
   thousands of men.
They all shook their heads and gave me a smile as though
   I was trying to fool with them.
And then one Sunday afternoon I wandered out along
   the Desplaines river
And I saw a crowd of Hungarians under the trees with
   their women and children and a keg of beer and an
   accordion.

MUCKERS

Twenty men stand watching the muckers.
    Stabbing the sides of the ditch
    Where clay gleams yellow,
    Driving the blades of their shovels
    Deeper and deeper for the new gas mains,
    Wiping sweat off their faces
       With red bandanas.
The muckers work on . . pausing . . to pull
Their boots out of suckholes where they slosh.

    Of the twenty looking on
Ten murmur, "O, it's a hell of a job,"
Ten others, "Jesus, I wish I had the job."

BLACKLISTED

Why shall I keep the old name?
What is a name anywhere anyway?
A name is a cheap thing all fathers and mothers leave
    each child:
A job is a job and I want to live, so
Why does God Almighty or anybody else care whether I
    take a new name to go by?

GRACELAND

Tomb of a millionaire,
A multimillionaire, ladies and gentlemen,
Place of the dead where they spend every year
The usury of twenty-five thousand dollars
    For upkeep and flowers
To keep fresh the memory of the dead.
The merchant prince gone to dust
Commanded in his written will
Over the signed name of his last testament
Twenty-five thousand dollars be set aside
For roses, lilacs, hydrangeas, tulips,
For perfume and color, sweetness of remembrance
Around his last long home.

(A hundred cash girls want nickels to go to the movies
    tonight.
In the back stalls of a hundred saloons, women are at
    tables
Drinking with men or waiting for men jingling loose
    silver dollars in their pockets.
In a hundred furnished rooms is a girl who sells silk or
    dress goods or leather stuff for six dollars a week
    wages
And when she pulls on her stockings in the morning she
    is reckless about God and the newspapers and the
    police, the talk of her home town or the name people
    call her.)

THE RIGHT TO GRIEF
To Certain Poets About to Die

Take your fill of intimate remorse, perfumed sorrow,
Over the dead child of a millionaire,
And the pity of Death refusing any check on the bank
Which the millionaire might order his secretary to scratch
off
And get cashed.

   Very well,
You for your grief and I for mine.
Let me have a sorrow my own if I want to.

I shall cry over the dead child of a stockyards hunky.
His job is sweeping blood off the floor.
He gets a dollar seventy cents a day when he works
And it's many tubs of blood he shoves out with a broom
day by day.

Now his three-year-old daughter
Is in a white coffin that cost him a week's wages.
Every Saturday night he will pay the undertaker fifty
cents till the debt is wiped out.

The hunky and his wife and the kids
Cry over the pinched face almost at peace in the white
box.
They remember it was scrawny and ran up high doctor
bills.
They are glad it is gone for the rest of the family now will
have more to eat and wear.

Yet before the majesty of Death they cry around the
    coffin
And wipe their eyes with red bandanas and sob when the
    priest says, "God have mercy on us all."

I have a right to feel my throat choke about this.
You take your grief and I mine—see?
Tomorrow there is no funeral and the hunky goes back to
    his job sweeping blood off the floor at a dollar sev-
    enty cents a day.
All he does all day long is keep on shoving hog blood
    ahead of him with a broom.

CHILD OF THE ROMANS

The dago shovelman sits by the railroad track
Eating a noon meal of bread and bologna.
    A train whirls by, and men and women at tables
    Alive with red roses and yellow jonquils,
    Eat steaks running with brown gravy,
    Strawberries and cream, eclairs and coffee.
The dago shovelman finishes the dry bread and bologna,
Washes it down with a dipper from the water-boy,
And goes back to the second half of a ten-hour day's
    work
Keeping the roadbed so the roses and jonquils
Shake hardly at all in the cut glass vases
Standing slender on the tables in the dining cars.

MAG

I wish to God I never saw you, Mag.
I wish you never quit your job and came along with me.
I wish we never bought a license and a white dress
For you to get married in the day we ran off to a minister
And told him we would love each other and take care of
    each other
Always and always long as the sun and the rain lasts
    anywhere.
Yes, I'm wishing now you lived somewhere away from
    here
And I was a bum on the bumpers a thousand miles away
    dead broke.
      I wish the kids had never come
      And rent and coal and clothes to pay for
      And a grocery man calling for cash,
      Every day cash for beans and prunes.
      I wish to God I never saw you, Mag.
      I wish to God the kids had never come.

ONION DAYS

Mrs. Gabrielle Giovannitti comes along Peoria Street
    every morning at nine o'clock
With kindling wood piled on top of her head, her eyes
    looking straight ahead to find the way for her old
    feet.
Her daughter-in-law, Mrs. Pietro Giovannitti, whose
    husband was killed in a tunnel explosion through the
    negligence of a fellow-servant,
Works ten hours a day, sometimes twelve, picking onions
    for Jasper on the Bowmanville road.
She takes a street car at half-past five in the morning,
    Mrs. Pietro Giovannitti does,
And gets back from Jasper's with cash for her day's work,
    between nine and ten o'clock at night.
Last week she got eight cents a box, Mrs. Pietro Giovan-
    nitti, picking onions for Jasper,
But this week Jasper dropped the pay to six cents a box
    because so many women and girls were answering
    the ads in the *Daily News*.
Jasper belongs to an Episcopal church in Ravenswood
    and on certain Sundays
He enjoys chanting the Nicene creed with his daughters
    on each side of him joining their voices with his.
If the preacher repeats old sermons of a Sunday, Jasper's
    mind wanders to his 700-acre farm and how he can
    make it produce more efficiently
And sometimes he speculates on whether he could word
    an ad in the *Daily News* so it would bring more
    women and girls out to his farm and reduce operat-
    ing costs.
Mrs. Pietro Giovannitti is far from desperate about life;
    her joy is in a child she knows will arrive to her in
    three months.

And now while these are the pictures for today there are
other pictures of the Giovannitti people I could give
you for tomorrow,
And how some of them go to the county agent on winter
mornings with their baskets for beans and cornmeal
and molasses.
I listen to fellows saying here's good stuff for a novel or
it might be worked up into a good play.
I say there's no dramatist living can put old Mrs. Gabrielle Giovannitti into a play with that kindling
wood piled on top of her head coming along Peoria
Street nine o'clock in the morning.

POPULATION DRIFTS

New-mown hay smell and wind of the plain made her a
    woman whose ribs had the power of the hills in them
    and her hands were tough for work and there was
    passion for life in her womb.
She and her man crossed the ocean and the years that
    marked their faces saw them haggling with land-
    lords and grocers while six children played on the
    stones and prowled in the garbage cans.
One child coughed its lungs away, two more have ade-
    noids and can neither talk nor run like their mother,
    one is in jail, two have jobs in a box factory
And as they fold the pasteboard, they wonder what the
    wishing is and the wistful glory in them that flutters
    faintly when the glimmer of spring comes on the air
    or the green of summer turns brown:
They do not know it is the new-mown hay smell calling
    and the wind of the plain praying for them to come
    back and take hold of life again with tough hands
    and with passion.

CRIPPLE

Once when I saw a cripple
Gasping slowly his last days with the white plague,
Looking from hollow eyes, calling for air,
Desperately gesturing with wasted hands
In the dark and dust of a house down in a slum,
I said to myself
I would rather have been a tall sunflower
Living in a country garden
Lifting a golden-brown face to the summer,
Rain-washed and dew-misted,
Mixed with the poppies and ranking hollyhocks,
And wonderingly watching night after night
The clear silent processionals of stars.

A FENCE

Now the stone house on the lake front is finished and the
workmen are beginning the fence.
The palings are made of iron bars with steel points that
can stab the life out of any man who falls on them.
As a fence, it is a masterpiece, and will shut off the rabble
and all vagabonds and hungry men and all wandering children looking for a place to play.
Passing through the bars and over the steel points will go
nothing except Death and the Rain and Tomorrow.

ANNA IMROTH

Cross the hands over the breast here—so.
Straighten the legs a little more—so.
And call for the wagon to come and take her home.
Her mother will cry some and so will her sisters and
     brothers.
But all of the others got down and they are safe and this
     is the only one of the factory girls who wasn't lucky
     in making the jump when the fire broke.
It is the hand of God and the lack of fire escapes.

WORKING GIRLS

The working girls in the morning are going to work—long lines of them afoot amid the downtown stores and factories, thousands with little brick-shaped lunches wrapped in newspapers under their arms.

Each morning as I move through this river of young-woman life I feel a wonder about where it is all going, so many with a peach bloom of young years on them and laughter of red lips and memories in their eyes of dances the night before and plays and walks.

Green and gray streams run side by side in a river and so here are always the others, those who have been over the way, the women who know each one the end of life's gamble for her, the meaning and the clew, the how and the why of the dances and the arms that passed around their waists and the fingers that played in their hair.

Faces go by written over: "I know it all, I know where the bloom and the laughter go and I have memories," and the feet of these move slower and they have wisdom where the others have beauty.

So the green and the gray move in the early morning on the downtown streets.

MAMIE

Mamie beat her head against the bars of a little Indiana
    town and dreamed of romance and big things off
    somewhere the way the railroad trains all ran.
She could see the smoke of the engines get lost down
    where the streaks of steel flashed in the sun and
    when the newspapers came in on the morning mail
    she knew there was a big Chicago far off, where all
    the trains ran.
She got tired of the barber shop boys and the post office
    chatter and the church gossip and the old pieces the
    band played on the Fourth of July and Decoration
    Day
And sobbed at her fate and beat her head against the
    bars and was going to kill herself
When the thought came to her that if she was going to die
    she might as well die struggling for a clutch of ro-
    mance among the streets of Chicago.
She has a job now at six dollars a week in the basement
    of the Boston Store
And even now she beats her head against the bars in the
    same old way and wonders if there is a bigger place
    the railroads run to from Chicago where maybe
    there is

                    romance
                    and big things
                    and real dreams
                    that never go smash.

PERSONALITY

*Musings of a Police Reporter in the
Identification Bureau*

You have loved forty women, but you have only one
thumb.

You have led a hundred secret lives, but you mark only
one thumb.

You go round the world and fight in a thousand wars and
win all the world's honors, but when you come back
home the print of the one thumb your mother gave
you is the same print of thumb you had in the old
home when your mother kissed you and said good-
by.

Out of the whirling womb of time come millions of men
and their feet crowd the earth and they cut one
anothers' throats for room to stand and among them
all are not two thumbs alike.

Somewhere is a Great God of Thumbs who can tell the
inside story of this.

CUMULATIVES

Storms have beaten on this point of land
And ships gone to wreck here
        and the passers-by remember it
        with talk on the deck at night
        as they near it.

Fists have beaten on the face of this old prizefighter
And his battles have held the sporting pages
        and on the street they indicate him with their
        right forefinger as one who once wore
        a championship belt.

A hundred stories have been published and a thousand
    rumored
About why this tall dark man has divorced two beautiful
    young women
And married a third who resembles the first two
        and they shake their heads and say, "There he
            goes,"
        when he passes by in sunny weather or in rain
        along the city streets.

TO CERTAIN JOURNEYMEN

Undertakers, hearse drivers, grave diggers,
I speak to you as one not afraid of your business.

You handle dust going to a long country,
You know the secret behind your job is the same whether
    you lower the coffin with modern, automatic ma-
    chinery, well-oiled and noiseless, or whether the
    body is laid in by naked hands and then covered by
    the shovels.

Your day's work is done with laughter many days of the
    year,
And you earn a living by those who say good-by today in
    thin whispers.

CHAMFORT

There's Chamfort. He's a sample.
Locked himself in his library with a gun,
Shot off his nose and shot out his right eye.
And this Chamfort knew how to write
And thousands read his books on how to live,
But he himself didn't know
How to die by force of his own hand—see?
They found him a red pool on the carpet
Cool as an April forenoon,
Talking and talking gay maxïms and grim epigrams.

Well, he wore bandages over his nose and right eye,
Drank coffee and chatted many years
With men and women who loved him
Because he laughed and daily dared Death:
"Come and take me."

LIMITED

I am riding on a limited express, one of the crack trains
 of the nation.
Hurtling across the prairie into blue haze and dark air go
 fifteen all-steel coaches holding a thousand people.
(All the coaches shall be scrap and rust and all the men
 and women laughing in the diners and sleepers shall
 pass to ashes.)
I ask a man in the smoker where he is going and he
 answers: "Omaha."

IN A BACK ALLEY

Remembrance for a great man is this.
The newsies are pitching pennies.
And on the copper disk is the man's face.
Dead lover of boys, what do you ask for now?

A COIN

Your western heads here cast on money,
You are the two that fade away together,
      Partners in the mist.

      Lunging buffalo shoulder,
      Lean Indian face,
We who come after where you are gone
Salute your forms on the new nickel.

      You are
      To us:
      The past.

      Runners
      On the prairie:
      Good-by.

DYNAMITER

I sat with a dynamiter at supper in a German saloon
    eating steak and onions.
And he laughed and told stories of his wife and children
    and the cause of labor and the working class.
It was laughter of an unshakable man knowing life to be
    a rich and red-blooded thing.
Yes, his laugh rang like the call of gray birds filled with
    a glory of joy ramming their winged flight through a
    rainstorm.
His name was in many newspapers as an enemy of the
    nation and few keepers of churches or schools would
    open their doors to him.
Over the steak and onions not a word was said of his deep
    days and nights as a dynamiter.
Only I always remember him as a lover of life, a lover of
    children, a lover of all free, reckless laughter every-
    where—lover of red hearts and red blood the world
    over.

ICE HANDLER

I know an ice handler who wears a flannel shirt with
    pearl buttons the size of a dollar,
And he lugs a hundred-pound hunk into a saloon icebox,
    helps himself to cold ham and rye bread,
Tells the bartender it's hotter than yesterday and will be
    hotter yet tomorrow, by Jesus,
And is on his way with his head in the air and a hard pair
    of fists.
He spends a dollar or so every Saturday night on a two-
    hundred-pound woman who washes dishes in the
    Hotel Morrison.
He remembers when the union was organized he broke
    the noses of two scabs and loosened the nuts so the
    wheels came off six different wagons one morning,
    and he came around and watched the ice melt in the
    street.
All he was sorry for was one of the scabs bit him on the
    knuckles of the right hand so they bled when he
    came around to the saloon to tell the boys about it.

JACK

Jack was a swarthy, swaggering son-of-a-gun.

He worked thirty years on the railroad, ten hours a day,
and his hands were tougher than sole leather.

He married a tough woman and they had eight children
and the women died and the children grew up and
went away and wrote the old man every two years.

He died in the poorhouse sitting on a bench in the sun
telling reminiscences to other old men whose
women were dead and children scattered.

There was joy on his face when he died as there was joy
on his face when he lived—he was a swarthy, swaggering son-of-a-gun.

FELLOW CITIZENS

I drank musty ale at the Illinois Athletic Club with the
    millionaire manufacturer of Green River butter one
    night
And his face had the shining light of an old-time Quaker,
    he spoke of a beautiful daughter, and I knew he had
    a peace and a happiness up his sleeve somewhere.
Then I heard Jim Kirch make a speech to the Advertising
    Association on the trade resources of South America.
And the way he lighted a three-for-a-nickel stogie and
    cocked it at an angle regardless of the manners of
    our best people,
I knew he had a clutch on a real happiness even though
    some of the reporters on his newspaper say he is the
    living double of Jack London's Sea Wolf.
In the mayor's office the mayor himself told me he was
    happy though it is a hard job to satisfy all the of-
    fice-seekers and eat all the dinners he is asked to eat.
Down in Gilpin Place, near Hull House, was a man with
    his jaw wrapped for a bad toothache,
And he had it all over the butter millionaire, Jim Kirch
    and the mayor when it came to happiness.
He is a maker of accordions and guitars and not only
    makes them from start to finish, but plays them after
    he makes them.
And he had a guitar of mahogany with a walnut bottom
    he offered for seven dollars and a half if I wanted it,
And another just like it, only smaller, for six dollars,
    though he never mentioned the price till I asked
    him,
And he stated the price in a sorry way, as though the
    music and the make of an instrument count for a
    million times more than the price in money.

I thought he had a real soul and knew a lot about God.

There was light in his eyes of one who has conquered
sorrow in so far as sorrow is conquerable or worth
conquering.

Anyway he is the only Chicago citizen I was jealous of
that day.

He played a dance they play in some parts of Italy when
the harvest of grapes is over and the wine presses
are ready for work.

TWO NEIGHBORS

Faces of two eternities keep looking at me.
One is Omar Khayam and the red stuff
    wherein men forget yesterday and tomorrow
    and remember only the voices and songs,
    the stories, newspapers and fights of today.
One is Louis Cornaro and a slim trick
    of slow, short meals across slow, short years,
    letting Death open the door only in slow, short
        inches.
I have a neighbor who swears by Omar.
I have a neighbor who swears by Cornaro.
                    Both are happy.
Faces of two eternities keep looking at me.
                    Let them look.

STYLE

Style—go ahead talking about style.
You can tell where a man gets his style just
    as you can tell where Pavlowa got her legs
    or Ty Cobb his batting eye.

    Go on talking.
Only don't take my style away.
      It's my face.
      Maybe no good
          but anyway, my face.
I talk with it, I sing with it, I see, taste and feel with it,
    I know why I want to keep it.

Kill my style
          and you break Pavlowa's legs,
          and you blind Ty Cobb's batting eye.

TO BEACHEY, 1912

Riding against the east,
A veering, steady shadow
Purrs the motor-call
Of the man-bird
Ready with the death-laughter
In his throat
And in his heart always
The love of the big blue beyond.

Only a man,
A far fleck of shadow on the east
Sitting at ease
With his hands on a wheel
And around him the large gray wings.
Hold him, great soft wings,
Keep and deal kindly, O wings,
With the cool, calm shadow at the wheel.

UNDER A HAT RIM

While the hum and the hurry
Of passing footfalls
Beat in my ear like the restless surf
Of a wind-blown sea,
A soul came to me
Out of the look on a face.

Eyes like a lake
Where a storm-wind roams
Caught me from under
The rim of a hat.
      I thought of a midsea wreck
      and bruised fingers clinging
      to a broken stateroom door.

IN A BREATH

To the Williamson Brothers

High noon. White sun flashes on the Michigan Avenue
asphalt. Drum of hoofs and whirr of motors. Women
trapsing along in flimsy clothes catching play of sun-
fire to their skin and eyes.

Inside the playhouse are movies from under the sea.
From the heat of pavements and the dust of sidewalks, passersby go in a breath to be witnesses of
large cool sponges, large cool fishes, large cool valleys and ridges of coral spread silent in the soak of
the ocean floor thousands of years.

A naked swimmer dives. A knife in his right hand shoots
a streak at the throat of a shark. The tail of the shark
lashes. One swing would kill the swimmer. . . . Soon
the knife goes into the soft underneck of the veering
fish. . . . Its mouthful of teeth, each tooth a dagger
itself, set row on row, glistens when the shuddering,
yawning cadaver is hauled up by the brothers of the
swimmer.

Outside in the street is the murmur and singing of life in
the sun—horses, motors, women trapsing along in
flimsy clothes, play of sun-fire in their blood.

BATH

A man saw the whole world as a grinning skull and crossbones. The rose flesh of life shriveled from all faces. Nothing counts. Everything is a fake. Dust to dust and ashes to ashes and then an old darkness and a useless silence. So he saw it all. Then he went to a Mischa Elman concert. Two hours waves of sound beat on his eardrums. Music washed something or other inside him. Music broke down and rebuilt something or other in his head and heart. He joined in five encores for the young Russian Jew with the fiddle. When he got outside his heels hit the sidewalk a new way. He was the same man in the same world as before. Only there was a singing fire and a climb of roses everlastingly over the world he looked on.

BRONZES

I

The bronze General Grant riding a bronze horse in Lincoln Park
Shrivels in the sun by day when the motor cars whirr by
in long processions going somewhere to keep ap-
pointments for dinner and matineés and buying and
selling
Though in the dusk and nightfall when high waves are
piling
On the slabs of the promenade along the lake shore near
by
I have seen the general dare the combers come closer
And make to ride his bronze horse out into the hoofs and
guns of the storm.

II

I cross Lincoln Park on a winter night when the snow is
falling.
Lincoln in bronze stands among the white lines of snow,
his bronze forehead meeting soft echoes of the newsies crying forty thousand men are dead along the
Yser, his bronze ears listening to the mumbled roar
of the city at his bronze feet.
A lithe Indian on a bronze pony, Shakespeare seated with
long legs in bronze, Garibaldi in a bronze cape, they
hold places in the cold, lonely snow tonight on their
pedestals and so they will hold them past midnight
and into the dawn.

DUNES

What do we see here in the sand dunes of the white moon
    alone with our thoughts, Bill,
Alone with our dreams, Bill, soft as the women tying
    scarves around their heads dancing,
Alone with a picture and a picture coming one after the
    other of all the dead,
The dead more than all these grains of sand one by one
    piled here in the moon,
Piled against the skyline taking shapes like the hand of
    the wind wanted,
What do we see here, Bill, outside of what the wise men
    beat their heads on,
Outside of what the poets cry for and the soldiers drive
    on headlong and leave their skulls in the sun for—
    what, Bill?

ON THE WAY

Little one, you have been buzzing in the books,
Flittering in the newspapers and drinking beer with lawyers
And amid the educated men of the clubs you have been
getting an earful of speech from trained tongues.
Take an earful from me once, go with me on a hike
Along sand stretches on the great inland sea here
And while the eastern breeze blows on us and the restless
surge
Of the lake waves on the breakwater breaks with an ever
fresh monotone,
Let us ask ourselves: What is truth? what do you or I
know?
How much do the wisest of the world's men know about
where the massed human procession is going?

You have heard the mob laughed at?
I ask you: Is not the mob rough as the mountains are
rough?
And all things human rise from the mob and relapse and
rise again as rain to the sea?

READY TO KILL

Ten minutes now I have been looking at this.
I have gone by here before and wondered about it.
This is a bronze memorial of a famous general
Riding horseback with a flag and a sword and a revolver
    on him.
I want to smash the whole thing into a pile of junk to be
    hauled away to the scrap yard.
I put it straight to you,
After the farmer, the miner, the shop man, the factory
    hand, the fireman and the teamster,
Have all been remembered with bronze memorials,
Shaping them on the job of getting all of us
Something to eat and something to wear,
When they stack a few silhouettes
        Against the sky
        Here in the park,
And show the real huskies that are doing the work of the
    world, and feeding people instead of butchering
    them,
Then maybe I will stand here
And look easy at this general of the army holding a flag
    in the air,
And riding like hell on horseback
Ready to kill anybody that gets in his way,
Ready to run the red blood and slush the bowels of men
    all over the sweet new grass of the prairie.

TO A CONTEMPORARY BUNKSHOOTER

You come along . . . tearing your shirt . . . yelling about
Jesus.
Where do you get that stuff?
What do you know about Jesus?
Jesus had a way of talking soft and outside of a few
bankers and higher-ups among the con men of Jerusalem everybody liked to have this Jesus around
because he never made any fake passes and everything he said went and he helped the sick and gave
the people hope.

You come along squirting words at us, shaking your fist
and calling us all dam fools so fierce the froth slob-
bers over your lips . . . always blabbing we're all
going to hell straight off and you know all about it.

I've read Jesus' words. I know what he said. You don't
throw any scare into me. I've got your number. I
know how much you know about Jesus.
He never came near clean people or dirty people but
they felt cleaner because he came along. It was your
crowd of bankers and businessmen and lawyers
hired the sluggers and murderers who put Jesus out
of the running.

I say the same bunch backing you nailed the nails into the
hands of this Jesus of Nazareth. He had lined up
against him the same crooks and strong-arm men
now lined up with you paying your way.

This Jesus was good to look at, smelled good, listened
good. He threw out something fresh and beautiful
from the skin of his body and the touch of his hands
wherever he passed along.

You slimy bunkshooter, you put a smut on every human
   blossom in reach of your rotten breath belching
   about hell-fire and hiccupping about this Man who
   lived a clean life in Galilee.

When are you going to quit making the carpenters build
   emergency hospitals for women and girls driven
   crazy with wrecked nerves from your gibberish
   about Jesus—I put it to you again: Where do you get
   that stuff; what do you know about Jesus?

Go ahead and bust all the chairs you want to. Smash a
   whole wagonload of furniture at every performance.
   Turn sixty somersaults and stand on your nutty
   head. If it wasn't for the way you scare the women
   and kids I'd feel sorry for you and pass the hat.
I like to watch a good four-flusher work, but not when he
   starts people puking and calling for the doctors.
I like a man that's got nerve and can pull off a great
   original performance, but you—you're only a bug-
   house peddler of second-hand gospel—you're only
   shoving out a phoney imitation of the goods this
   Jesus wanted free as air and sunlight.

You tell people living in shanties Jesus is going to fix it up
   all right with them by giving them mansions in the
   skies after they're dead and the worms have eaten
   'em.
You tell $6 a week department store girls all they need is
   Jesus; you take a steel trust wop, dead without having lived, gray and shrunken at forty years of age,
   and you tell him to look at Jesus on the cross and
   he'll be all right.
You tell poor people they don't need any more money on
   pay day and even if it's fierce to be out of a job,
   Jesus'll fix that up all right, all right—all they gotta
   do is take Jesus the way you say.

I'm telling you Jesus wouldn't stand for the stuff you're
handing out. Jesus played it different. The bankers
and lawyers of Jerusalem got their sluggers and murderers to go after Jesus just because Jesus wouldn't
play their game. He didn't sit in with the big thieves.

I don't want a lot of gab from a bunkshooter in my
religion.
I won't take my religion from any man who never works
except with his mouth and never cherishes any
memory except the face of the woman on the American silver dollar.

I ask you to come through and show me where you're
pouring out the blood of your life.
I've been to this suburb of Jerusalem they call Golgotha,
where they nailed Him, and I know if the story is
straight it was real blood ran from His hands and the
nail-holes, and it was real blood spurted in red drops
where the spear of the Roman soldier rammed in
between the ribs of this Jesus of Nazareth.

SKYSCRAPER

By day the skyscraper looms in the smoke and sun and
    has a soul.
Prairie and valley, streets of the city, pour people into it
    and they mingle among its twenty floors and are
    poured out again back to the streets, prairies and
    valleys.
It is the men and women, boys and girls so poured in and
    out all day that give the building a soul of dreams
    and thoughts and memories.
(Dumped in the sea or fixed in a desert, who would care
    for the building or speak its name or ask a policeman
    the way to it?)

Elevators slide on their cables and tubes catch letters and
    parcels and iron pipes carry gas and water in and
    sewage out.
Wires climb with secrets, carry light and carry words,
    and tell terrors and profits and loves—curses of men
    grappling plans of business and questions of women
    in plots of love.

Hour by hour the caissons reach down to the rock of the
    earth and hold the building to a turning planet.
Hour by hour the girders play as ribs and reach out and
    hold together the stone walls and floors.
Hour by hour the hand of the mason and the stuff of the
    mortar clinch the pieces and parts to the shape an
    architect voted.
Hour by hour the sun and the rain, the air and the rust,
    and the press of time running into centuries, play on
    the building inside and out and use it.

Men who sunk the pilings and mixed the mortar are laid
in graves where the wind whistles a wild song without words

And so are men who strung the wires and fixed the pipes
and tubes and those who saw it rise floor by floor.

Souls of them all are here, even the hod carrier begging
at back doors hundreds of miles away and the bricklayer who went to state's prison for shooting another
man while drunk.

(One man fell from a girder and broke his neck at the end
of a straight plunge—he is here—his soul has gone
into the stones of the building.)

On the office doors from tier to tier—hundreds of names
and each name standing for a face written across
with a dead child, a passionate lover, a driving ambi-
tion for a million-dollar business or a lobster's ease
of life.

Behind the signs on the doors they work and the walls tell
nothing from room to room.

Ten-dollar-a-week stenographers take letters from corporation officers, lawyers, efficiency engineers, and
tons of letters go bundled from the building to all
ends of the earth.

Smiles and tears of each office girl go into the soul of the
building just the same as the master-men who rule
the building.

Hands of clocks turn to noon hours and each floor empties
its men and women who go away and eat and come
back to work.

Toward the end of the afternoon all work slackens and all
jobs go slower as the people feel day closing on
them.

One by one the floors are emptied. . . . The uniformed elevator men are gone. Pails clang . . . Scrubbers work, talking in foreign tongues. Broom and water and mop clean from the floors human dust and spit, and machine grime of the day.

Spelled in electric fire on the roof are words telling miles of houses and people where to buy a thing for money. The sign speaks till midnight.

Darkness on the hallways. Voices echo. Silence holds. . . . Watchmen walk slow from floor to floor and try the doors. Revolvers bulge from their hip pockets. . . . Steel safes stand in corners. Money is stacked in them.

A young watchman leans at a window and sees the lights of barges butting their way across a harbor, nets of red and white lanterns in a railroad yard, and a span of glooms splashed with lines of white and blurs of crosses and clusters over the sleeping city.

By night the skyscraper looms in the smoke and the stars and has a soul.

Handfuls

FOG

The fog comes
on little cat feet.

It sits looking
over harbor and city
on silent haunches
and then moves on.

POOL

Out of the fire
Came a man sunken
To less than cinders,
A tea-cup of ashes or so.
And I,
The gold in the house,
Writhed into a stiff pool.

JAN KUBELIK

Your bow swept over a string, and a long low note quiv-
ered to the air.
(A mother of Bohemia sobs over a new child perfect
learning to suck milk.)

Your bow ran fast over all the high strings fluttering and
wild.
(All the girls in Bohemia are laughing on a Sunday afternoon in the hills with their lovers.)

CHOOSE

The single clenched fist lifted and ready,
Or the open asking hand held out and waiting.
Choose:
For we meet by one or the other.

CRIMSON

Crimson is the slow smolder of the cigar end I hold,
Gray is the ash that stiffens and covers all silent the fire.
(A great man I know is dead and while he lies in his coffin
    a gone flame I sit here in cumbering shadows and
    smoke and watch my thoughts come and go.)

WHITELIGHT

Your whitelight flashes the frost tonight
Moon of the purple and silent west.
Remember me one of your lovers of dreams.

FLUX

Sand of the sea runs red
Where the sunset reaches and quivers.
Sand of the sea runs yellow
Where the moon slants and wavers.

KIN

Brother, I am fire
Surging under the ocean floor.
I shall never meet you, brother—
Not for years, anyhow;
Maybe thousands of years, brother.
Then I will warm you,
Hold you close, wrap you in circles,
Use you and change you—
Maybe thousands of years, brother.

WHITE SHOULDERS

Your white shoulders
    I remember
And your shrug of laughter.

    Low laughter
    Shaken slow
From your white shoulders.

LOSSES

I have love
And a child,
A banjo
And shadows.
(Losses of God,
All will go
And one day
We will hold
Only the shadows.)

TROTHS

Yellow dust on a bumble
    bee's wing,
Gray lights in a woman's
    asking eyes,
Red ruins in the changing
    sunset embers:
I take you and pile high
    the memories.
Death will break her claws
    on some I keep.

War Poems

(1914–1915)

KILLERS

I am singing to you
Soft as a man with a dead child speaks;
Hard as a man in handcuffs,
Held where he cannot move:

Under the sun
Are sixteen million men,
Chosen for shining teeth,
Sharp eyes, hard legs,
And a running of young warm blood in their wrists.

And a red juice runs on the green grass;
And a red juice soaks the dark soil.
And the sixteen million are killing . . . and killing and
    killing.

I never forget them day or night:
They beat on my head for memory of them;
They pound on my heart and I cry back to them,
To their homes and women, dreams and games.

I wake in the night and smell the trenches,
And hear the low stir of sleepers in lines—
Sixteen million sleepers and pickets in the dark:
Some of them long sleepers for always,
Some of them tumbling to sleep tomorrow for always,
Fixed in the drag of the world's heartbreak,
Eating and drinking, toiling . . . on a long job of killing.
    Sixteen million men.

AMONG THE RED GUNS

*After waking at dawn one morning when the wind
sang low among dry leaves in an elm*

Among the red guns,
In the hearts of soldiers
Running free blood
In the long, long campaign:
    Dreams go on.

Among the leather saddles,
In the heads of soldiers
Heavy in the wracks and kills
Of all straight fighting:
    Dreams go on.

Among the hot muzzles,
In the hands of soldiers
Brought from flesh-folds of women—
Soft amid the blood and crying—
In all your hearts and heads
Among the guns and saddles and muzzles:

    Dreams,
Dreams go on,
Out of the dead on their backs,
Broken and no use any more:
Dreams of the way and the end go on.

IRON

Guns,
Long, steel guns,
Pointed from the war ships
In the name of the war god.
Straight, shining, polished guns,
Clambered over with jackies in white blouses,
Glory of tan faces, tousled hair, white teeth,
Laughing lithe jackies in white blouses,
Sitting on the guns singing war songs, war chanties.

Shovels,
Broad, iron shovels,
Scooping out oblong vaults,
Loosening turf and leveling sod.

   I ask you
   To witness—
   The shovel is brother to the gun.

MURMURINGS IN A FIELD HOSPITAL

[They picked him up in the grass where he had lain
two days in the rain with a piece of shrapnel in
his lungs.]

Come to me only with playthings now . . .
A picture of a singing woman with blue eyes
Standing at a fence of hollyhocks, poppies and sun-
    flowers . . .
Or an old man I remember sitting with children telling
    stories
Of days that never happened anywhere in the world . . .

No more iron cold and real to handle,
Shaped for a drive straight ahead.
Bring me only beautiful useless things.
Only old home things touched at sunset in the quiet . . .
And at the window one day in summer
Yellow of the new crock of butter
Stood against the red of new climbing roses . . .
And the world was all playthings.

STATISTICS

Napoleon shifted,
Restless in the old sarcophagus
And murmured to a watchguard:
"Who goes there?"
"Twenty-one million men,
Soldiers, armies, guns,
Twenty-one million
A foot, horseback,
In the air,
Under the sea."
And Napoleon turned to his sleep:
"It is not my world answering;
It is some dreamer who knows not
The world I marched in
From Calais to Moscow."
And he slept on
In the old sarcophagus
While the aëroplanes
Droned their motors
Between Napoleon's mausoleum
And the cool night stars.

FIGHT

Red drips from my chin where I have been eating.
Not all the blood, nowhere near all, is wiped off my
    mouth.

Clots of red mess my hair
And the tiger, the buffalo, know how.

I was a killer.
        Yes, I am a killer.

I come from killing.
        I go to more.
I drive red joy ahead of me from killing.
Red gluts and red hungers run in the smears and
    juices of my inside bones:
The child cries for a suck mother and I cry for war.

BUTTONS

I have been watching the war map slammed up for ad-
    vertising in front of the newspaper office.
Buttons—red and yellow buttons—blue and black but-
    tons—are shoved back and forth across the map.

A laughing young man, sunny with freckles,
Climbs a ladder, yells a joke to somebody in the crowd,
And then fixes a yellow button one inch west
And follows the yellow button with a black button one
    inch west.

(Ten thousand men and boys twist on their bodies in a
    red soak along a river edge,
Gasping of wounds, calling for water, some rattling death
    in their throats.)
Who would guess what it cost to move two buttons one
    inch on the war map here in front of the newspaper
    office where the freckle-faced young man is laughing
    to us?

AND THEY OBEY

Smash down the cities.
Knock the walls to pieces.
Break the factories and cathedrals, warehouses
    and homes
Into loose piles of stone and lumber and black
    burnt wood:
      You are the soldiers and we command you.

Build up the cities.
Set up the walls again.
Put together once more the factories and cathe-
    drals, warehouses and homes
Into buildings for life and labor:
      You are workmen and citizens all: We com-
      mand you.

JAWS

Seven nations stood with their hands on the jaws of
    death.
It was the first week in August, Nineteen Hundred Four-
    teen.
I was listening, you were listening, the whole world was
    listening,
And all of us heard a Voice murmuring:
          "I am the way and the light,
          He that believeth on me
          Shall not perish
          But shall have everlasting life."
Seven nations listening heard the Voice and answered:
          "O Hell!"
The jaws of death began clicking and they go on clicking:
          "O Hell!"

SALVAGE

Guns on the battle lines have pounded now a year between Brussels and Paris.

And, William Morris, when I read your old chapter on
the great arches and naves and little whimsical corners of the Churches of Northern France—Brr-rr!

I'm glad you're a dead man, William Morris, I'm glad
you're down in the damp and moldy, only a memory
instead of a living man—I'm glad you're gone.

You never lied to us, William Morris, you loved the shape
of those stones piled and carved for you to dream
over and wonder because workmen got joy of life
into them,

Workmen in aprons singing while they hammered, and
praying, and putting their songs and prayers into the
walls and roofs, the bastions and cornerstones and
gargoyles—all their children and kisses of women
and wheat and roses growing.

I say, William Morris, I'm glad you're gone, I'm glad
you're a dead man.

Guns on the battle lines have pounded a year now between Brussels and Paris.

WARS

In the old wars drum of hoofs and the beat of shod feet.
In the new wars hum of motors and the tread of rubber tires.
In the wars to come silent wheels and whirr of rods not yet dreamed out in the heads of men.

In the old wars clutches of short swords and jabs into faces with spears.
In the new wars long-range guns and smashed walls, guns running a spit of metal and men falling in tens and twenties.
In the wars to come new silent deaths, new silent hurlers not yet dreamed out in the heads of men.

In the old wars kings quarreling and thousands of men following.
In the new wars kings quarreling and millions of men following.
In the wars to come kings kicked under the dust and millions of men following great causes not yet dreamed out in the heads of men.

The Road
and the End

THE ROAD AND THE END

I shall foot it
Down the roadway in the dusk,
Where shapes of hunger wander
And the fugitives of pain go by.
I shall foot it
In the silence of the morning,
See the night slur into dawn,
Hear the slow great winds arise
Where tall trees flank the way
And shoulder toward the sky.

The broken boulders by the road
Shall not commemorate my ruin.
Regret shall be the gravel under foot.
I shall watch for
Slim birds swift of wing
That go where wind and ranks of thunder
Drive the wild processionals of rain.

The dust of the traveled road
Shall touch my hands and face.

CHOICES

They offer you many things,
    I a few.
Moonlight on the play of fountains at night
With water sparkling a drowsy monotone,
Bare-shouldered, smiling women and talk
And a cross-play of loves and adulteries
And a fear of death
                and a remembering of regrets
All this they offer you.
I come with:
    salt and bread
    a terrible job of work
    and tireless war;
Come and have now:
    hunger.
    danger
    and hate.

GRAVES

I dreamed one man stood against a thousand,
One man damned as a wrongheaded fool.
One year and another he walked the streets,
And a thousand shrugs and hoots
Met him in the shoulders and mouths he passed.

    He died alone
And only the undertaker came to his funeral.

Flowers grow over his grave anod in the wind,
And over the graves of the thousand, too,
The flowers grow anod in the wind.

    Flowers and the wind,
Flowers anod over the graves of the dead,
Petals of red, leaves of yellow, streaks of white,
Masses of purple sagging . . .
I love you and your great way of forgetting.

AZTEC MASK

I wanted a man's face looking into the jaws and throat of
    life
With something proud on his face, so proud no smash of
    the jaws,
No gulp of the throat leaves the face in the end
With anything else than the old proud look:

> Even to the finish, dumped in the dust,
> Lost among the used-up cinders,
> This face, men would say, is a flash,
> Is laid on bones taken from the ribs of the earth,
> Ready for the hammers of changing, changing
>   years,
> Ready for the sleeping, sleeping years of
>   silence.
> Ready for the dust and fire and wind.

I wanted this face and I saw it today in an Aztec mask.
A cry out of storm and dark, a red yell and a purple
    prayer,
A beaten shape of ashes

>   waiting the sunrise or night,
>   something or nothing,
>   proud-mouthed,
>   proud-eyed gambler.

MOMUS

Momus is the name men give your face,
The brag of its tone, like a long low steamboat whistle
Finding a way mid mist on a shoreland,
Where gray rocks let the salt water shatter spray
Against horizons purple, silent.

Yes, Momus,
Men have flung your face in bronze
To gaze in gargoyle downward on a street-whirl of folk.
They were artists did this, shaped your sad mouth,
Gave you a tall forehead slanted with calm, broad wis-
dom;
All your lips to the corners and your cheeks to the high
bones
Thrown over and through with a smile that forever
wishes and wishes, purple, silent, fled from all the
iron things of life, evaded like a sought bandit, gone
into dreams, by God.

I wonder, Momus,
Whether shadows of the dead sit somewhere and look
with deep laughter
On men who play in terrible earnest the old, known,
solemn repetitions of history.
A droning monotone soft as sea laughter hovers from
your kindliness of bronze,
You give me the human ease of a mountain peak, purple,
silent;
Granite shoulders heaving above the earth curves,
Careless eye-witness of the spawning tides of men and
women
Swarming always in a drift of millions to the dust of toil,
the salt of tears,
And blood drops of undiminishing war.

THE ANSWER

You have spoken the answer.
A child searches far sometimes
Into the red dust
                On a dark rose leaf
And so you have gone far
                For the answer is:
                        Silence.

    In the republic
Of the winking stars
                and spent cataclysms
Sure we are it is off there the answer
      is hidden and folded over,
Sleeping in the sun, careless whether
      it is Sunday or any other day of
      the week,

Knowing silence will bring all one way
      or another.

Have we not seen
Purple of the pansy
            out of the mulch
            and mold
            crawl
            into a dusk
            of velvet?
            blur of yellow?
Almost we thought from nowhere but it was the
      silence,
            the future,
            working.

TO A DEAD MAN

Over the dead line we have called to you
To come across with a word to us,
Some beaten whisper of what happens
Where you are over the dead line
Deaf to our calls and voiceless.

The flickering shadows have not answered
Nor your lips sent a signal
Whether love talks and roses grow
And the sun breaks at morning
Splattering the sea with crimson.

UNDER

I

I am the undertow
Washing tides of power
Battering the pillars
Under your things of high law.

II

I am a sleepless
Slowfaring eater,
Maker of rust and rot
In your bastioned fastenings,
Caissons deep.

III

I am the Law
Older than you
And your builders proud.

I am deaf
In all days
Whether you
Say "Yes" or "No."

I am the crumbler:
Tomorrow.

A SPHINX

Close-mouthed you sat five thousand years and never let
out a whisper.
Processions came by, marchers, asking questions you answered with gray eyes never blinking, shut lips
never talking.
Not one croak of anything you know has come from your
cat crouch of ages.
I am one of those who know all you know and I keep my
questions: I know the answers you hold.

WHO AM I?

My head knocks against the stars.
My feet are on the hilltops.
My fingertips are in the valleys and shores of universal
    life.
Down in the sounding foam of primal things I reach my
    hands and play with pebbles of destiny.
I have been to hell and back many times.
I know all about heaven, for I have talked with God.
I dabble in the blood and guts of the terrible.
I know the passionate seizure of beauty
And the marvelous rebellion of man at all signs reading
    "Keep Off."

My name is Truth and I am the most elusive captive in
    the universe.

OUR PRAYER OF THANKS

For the gladness here where the sun is shining at evening
   on the weeds at the river,
   Our prayer of thanks.

For the laughter of children who tumble barefooted and
   bareheaded in the summer grass,
   Our prayer of thanks.

For the sunset and the stars, the women and the white
   arms that hold us,
   Our prayer of thanks.

   God,
If you are deaf and blind, if this is all lost to you,
God, if the dead in their coffins amid the silver handles
   on the edge of town, or the reckless dead of war days
   thrown unknown in pits, if these dead are forever
   deaf and blind and lost,
   Our prayer of thanks.

   God,
The game is all your way, the secrets and the signals and
   .the system; and so for the break of the game and the
   first play and the last.
Our prayer of thanks.

Fogs and
Fires

AT A WINDOW

Give me hunger,
O you gods that sit and give
The world its orders.
Give me hunger, pain and want,
Shut me out with shame and failure
From your doors of gold and fame,
Give me your shabbiest, weariest hunger!

But leave me a little love,
A voice to speak to me in the day end,
A hand to touch me in the dark room
Breaking the long loneliness.
In the dusk of day-shapes
Blurring the sunset,
One little wandering, western star
Thrust out from the changing shores of shadow.
Let me go to the window,
Watch there the day-shapes of dusk
And wait and know the coming
Of a little love.

UNDER THE
HARVEST MOON

Under the harvest moon,
When the soft silver
Drips shimmering
Over the garden nights,
Death, the gray mocker,
Comes and whispers to you
As a beautiful friend
Who remembers.

Under the summer roses
When the flagrant crimson
Lurks in the dusk
Of the wild red leaves,
Love, with little hands,
Comes and touches you
With a thousand memories,
And asks you
Beautiful, unanswerable questions.

THE GREAT HUNT

I cannot tell you now;
    When the wind's drive and whirl
    Blow me along no longer,
    And the wind's a whisper at last—
Maybe I'll tell you then—
                  some other time.

    When the rose's flash to the sunset
    Reels to the rack and the twist,
    And the rose is a red bygone,
    When the face I love is going
    And the gate to the end shall clang,
    And it's no use to beckon or say, "So long"—
Maybe I'll tell you then—
                  some other time.

I never knew any more beautiful than you:
    I have hunted you under my thoughts,
    I have broken down under the wind
    And into the roses looking for you.
      I shall never find any
                greater than you.

MONOTONE

The monotone of the rain is beautiful,
And the sudden rise and slow relapse
Of the long multitudinous rain.

The sun on the hills is beautiful,
Or a captured sunset sea-flung,
Bannered with fire and gold.

A face I know is beautiful—
With fire and gold of sky and sea,
And the peace of long warm rain.

JOY

Let a joy keep you.
Reach out your hands
And take it when it runs by,
As the Apache dancer
Clutches his woman.
I have seen them
Live long and laugh loud,
Sent on singing, singing,
Smashed to the heart
Under the ribs
With a terrible love.
Joy always,
Joy everywhere—
Let joy kill you!
Keep away from the little deaths.

SHIRT

I remember once I ran after you and tagged the fluttering
    shirt of you in the wind.
Once many days ago I drank a glassful of something and
    the picture of you shivered and slid on top of the
    stuff.
And again it was nobody else but you I heard in the
    singing voice of a careless humming woman.
One night when I sat with chums telling stories at a
    bonfire flickering red embers, in a language its own
    talking to a spread of white stars:
        It was you that slunk laughing
        in the clumsy staggering shadows.
Broken answers of remembrance let me know you are
    alive with a peering phantom face behind a doorway
    somewhere in the city's push and fury
Or under a pack of moss and leaves waiting in silence
    under a twist of oaken arms ready as ever to run
    away again when I tag the fluttering shirt of you.

AZTEC

You came from the Aztecs
With a copper on your forearms
Tawnier than a sunset
Saying good-by to an even river.

And I said, you remember,
Those forearms of yours
Were finer than bronzes
And you were glad.

                 It was tears
And a path west
         and a home-going
         when I asked
Why there were scars of worn gold
Where a man's ring was fixed once
On your third finger.
               And I call you
To come back
        before the days are longer.

TWO

Memory of you is . . . a blue spear of flower.
I cannot remember the name of it.
Alongside a bold dripping poppy is fire and silk.
And they cover you.

BACK YARD

Shine on, O moon of summer.
Shine to the leaves of grass, catalpa and oak,
All silver under your rain tonight.

An Italian boy is sending songs to you tonight from an
    accordion.
A Polish boy is out with his best girl; they marry next
    month; tonight they are throwing you kisses.

An old man next door is dreaming over a sheen that sits
    in a cherry tree in his back yard.

The clocks say I must go—I stay here sitting on the back
    porch drinking white thoughts you rain down.

    Shine on, O moon,
Shake out more and more silver changes.

ON THE BREAKWATER

On the breakwater in the summer dark, a man and a girl
    are sitting,
She across his knee and they are looking face into face
Talking to each other without words, singing rhythms in
    silence to each other.

A funnel of white ranges the blue dusk from an outgoing
    boat,
Playing its searchlight, puzzled, abrupt, over a streak of
    green,
And two on the breakwater keep their silence, she on his
    knee.

MASK

Fling your red scarf faster and faster, dancer.
It is summer and the sun loves a million green leaves,
    masses of green.
Your red scarf flashes across them calling and a-calling.
The silk and flare of it is a great soprano leading a chorus
Carried along in a rouse of voices reaching for the heart
    of the world.
Your toes are singing to meet the song of your arms:

Let the red scarf go swifter.
Summer and the sun command you.

PEARL FOG

Open the door now.
Go roll up the collar of your coat
To walk in the changing scarf of mist.

Tell your sins here to the pearl fog
And know for once a deepening night
Strange as the half-meanings
Alurk in a wise woman's mousey eyes.

Yes, tell your sins
And know how careless a pearl fog is
Of the laws you have broken.

I SANG

I sang to you and the moon
But only the moon remembers.
   I sang
O reckless free-hearted
          free-throated rhythms,
Even the moon remembers them
And is kind to me.

FOLLIES

Shaken,
The blossoms of lilac,
   And shattered,
The atoms of purple.
Green dip the leaves,
   Darker the bark,
Longer the shadows.

Sheer lines of poplar
Shimmer with masses of silver
And down in a garden old with years
And broken walls of ruin and story,
Roses rise with red rain-memories.
         May!
   In the open world
The sun comes and finds your face,
   Remembering all.

JUNE

Paula is digging and shaping the loam of a salvia,
  Scarlet Chinese talker of summer.
Two petals of crabapple blossom blow fallen in Paula's
    hair,
  And fluff of white from a cottonwood.

NOCTURNE IN A
DESERTED BRICKYARD

Stuff of the moon
Runs on the lapping sand
Out to the longest shadows.
Under the curving willows,
And round the creep of the wave line,
Fluxions of yellow and dusk on the waters
Make a wide dreaming pansy of an old pond in the night.

HYDRANGEAS

Dragoons, I tell you the white hydrangeas
    turn rust and go soon.
Already mid September a line of brown runs
    over them.
One sunset after another tracks the faces, the
    petals.
Waiting, they look over the fence for what
    way they go.

THEME IN YELLOW

I spot the hills
With yellow balls in autumn.
I light the prairie cornfields
Orange and tawny gold clusters
And I am called pumpkins.
On the last of October
When dusk is fallen
Children join hands
And circle round me
Singing ghost songs
And love to the harvest moon;
I am a jack-o'-lantern
With terrible teeth
And the children know
I am fooling.

BETWEEN TWO HILLS

Between two hills
The old town stands.
The houses loom
And the roofs and trees
And the dusk and the dark,
The damp and the dew
   Are there.

The prayers are said
And the people rest
For sleep is there
And the touch of dreams
   Is over all.

LAST ANSWERS

I wrote a poem on the mist
And a woman asked me what I meant by it.
I had thought till then only of the beauty of the mist, how
    pearl and gray of it mix and reel,
And change the drab shanties with lighted lamps at eve-
    ning into points of mystery quivering with color.

  I answered:
The whole world was mist once long ago and some day
    it will all go back to mist,
Our skulls and lungs are more water than bone and tissue
And all poets love dust and mist because all the last
    answers
Go running back to dust and mist.

WINDOW

Night from a railroad car window
Is a great, dark, soft thing
Broken across with slashes of light.

YOUNG SEA

The sea is never still.
It pounds on the shore
Restless as a young heart,
Hunting.

The sea speaks
And only the stormy hearts
Know what it says:
It is the face
        of a rough mother speaking.

The sea is young.
One storm cleans all the hoar
And loosens the age of it.
I hear it laughing, reckless.

They love the sea,
Men who ride on it
And know they will die
Under the salt of it

Let only the young come,
   Says the sea.
Let them kiss my face
   And hear me.
I am the last word
   And I tell
Where storms and stars come from.

BONES

Sling me under the sea.
Pack me down in the salt and wet.
No farmer's plow shall touch my bones.
No Hamlet hold my jaws and speak
How jokes are gone and empty is my mouth.
Long, green-eyed scavengers shall pick my eyes,
Purple fish play hide-and-seek,
And I shall be song of thunder, crash of sea,
Down on the floors of salt and wet.
     Sling me . . . under the sea.

PALS

Take a hold now
On the silver handles here,
Six silver handles,
One for each of his old pals.

Take hold
And lift him down the stairs,
Put him on the rollers
Over the floor of the hearse.

Take him on the last haul,
To the cold straight house,
the level even house,
To the last house of all.

The dead say nothing
And the dead know much
And the dead hold under their tongues
A locked-up story.

CHILD

The young child, Christ, is straight and wise
And asks questions of the old men, questions
Found under running water for all children
And found under shadows thrown on still waters
By tall trees looking downward, old and gnarled.
Found to the eyes of children alone, untold,
Singing a low song in the loneliness.
And the young child, Christ, goes on asking
And the old men answer nothing and only know love
For the young child. Christ, straight and wise.

POPPIES

She loves blood-red poppies for a garden to walk in.
In a loose white gown she walks
        and a new child tugs at cords in her body.
Her head to the west at evening when the dew is
      creeping,
A shudder of gladness runs in her bones and torsal fiber:
She loves blood-red poppies for a garden to walk in.

CHILD MOON

The child's wonder
At the old moon
Comes back nightly.
She points her finger
To the far silent yellow thing
Shining through the branches
Filtering on the leaves a golden sand,
Crying with her little tongue, "See the moon!"
And in her bed fading to sleep
With babblings of the moon on her little mouth.

MARGARET

Many birds and the beating of wings
Make a flinging reckless hum
In the early morning at the rocks
Above the blue pool
Where the gray shadows swim lazy.

In your blue eyes, O reckless child,
I saw today many little wild wishes,
Eager as the great morning.

Shadows

IT IS MUCH

Women of night life amid the lights
Where the line of your full, round throats
Matches in gleam the glint of your eyes
And the ring of your heart-deep laughter:
   It is much to be warm and sure of tomorrow.

Women of night life along the shadows,
Lean at your throats and skulking the walls,
Gaunt as a bitch worn to the bone,
Under the paint of your smiling faces:
   It is much to be warm and sure of tomorrow.

POEMS DONE ON A
LATE NIGHT CAR

I. CHICKENS

I am The Great White Way of the city:
When you ask what is my desire, I answer:
"Girls fresh as country wild flowers,
With young faces tired of the cows and barns,
Eager in their eyes as the dawn to find my mysteries,
Slender supple girls with shapely legs,
Lure in the arch of their little shoulders
And wisdom from the prairies to cry only softly at the
    ashes of my mysteries."

II. USED UP

*Lines based on certain regrets that come with
rumination upon the painted faces of women
on North Clark Street, Chicago*

Roses,
Red roses,
Crushed
In the rain and wind
Like mouths of women
Beaten by the fists of
Men using them.
    O little roses
    And broken leaves
    And petal wisps:
You that so flung your crimson
    To the sun
Only yesterday.

III. HOME

Here is a thing my heart wishes the world had more of:
I heard it in the air of one night when I listened
To a mother singing softly to a child restless and angry in
the darkness.

TRAFFICKER

Among the shadows where two streets cross,
A woman lurks in the dark and waits
To move on when a policeman heaves in view.
Smiling a broken smile from a face
Painted over haggard bones and desperate eyes,
All night she offers passers-by what they will
Of her beauty wasted, body faded, claims gone,
And no takers.

HARRISON STREET COURT

I heard a woman's lips
Speaking to a companion
Say these words:

"A woman what hustles
Never keeps nothin'
For all her hustlin'.
Somebody always gets
What she goes on the street for.
If it ain't a pimp
It's a bull what gets it.
I been hustlin' now
Till I ain't much good any more.
I got nothin' to show for it.
Some man got it all,
Every night's hustlin' I ever did."

SOILED DOVE

Let us be honest; the lady was not a harlot until she
married a corporation lawyer who picked her from a
Ziegfeld chorus.

Before then she never took anybody's money and paid for
her silk stockings out of what she earned singing and
dancing.

She loved one man and he loved six women and the game
was changing her looks, calling for more and more
massage money and high coin for the beauty doctors.

Now she drives a long, underslung motor car all by her-
self, reads in the day's papers what her husband is
doing to the inter-state commerce commission, re-
quires a larger corsage from year to year, and won-
ders sometimes how one man is coming along with
six women.

JUNGHEIMER'S

In western fields of corn and northern timber lands,
    They talk about me, a saloon with a soul,
    The soft red lights, the long curving bar,
    The leather seats and dim corners,
    Tall brass spittoons, a nigger cutting ham,
And the painting of a woman half-dressed thrown reck-
    less across a bed after a night of booze and riots.

GONE

Everybody loved Chick Lorimer in our town.
                    Far off
          Everybody loved her.
So we all love a wild girl keeping a hold
          On a dream she wants.
Nobody knows now where Chick Lorimer went.
Nobody knows why she packed her trunk . . . a few
     old things
And is gone,
                    Gone with her little chin
                    Thrust ahead of her
                    And her soft hair blowing careless
                    From under a wide hat,
Dancer, singer, a laughing passionate lover.

Were there ten men or a hundred hunting Chick?
Were there five men or fifty with aching hearts?
          Everybody loved Chick Lorimer.
          Nobody knows where she's gone.

Other Days
(1900–1910)

DREAMS IN THE DUSK

Dreams in the dusk,
Only dreams closing the day
And with the day's close going back
To the gray things, the dark things,
The far, deep things of dreamland.

Dreams, only dreams in the dusk,
Only the old remembered pictures
Of lost days when the day's loss
Wrote in tears the heart's loss.

Tears and loss and broken dreams
May find your heart at dusk.

DOCKS

Strolling along
By the teeming docks,
I watch the ships put out.
Black ships that heave and lunge
And move like mastodons
Arising from lethargic sleep.

The fathomed harbor
Calls them not nor dares
Them to a strain of action,
But outward, on and outward,
Sounding low-reverberating calls,
Shaggy in the half-lit distance,
They pass the pointed headland,
View the wide, far-lifting wilderness
And leap with cumulative speed
To test the challenge of the sea.

Plunging,
Doggedly onward plunging,
Into salt and mist and foam and sun.

ALL DAY LONG

All day long in fog and wind,
The waves have flung their beating crests
Against the palisades of adamant.
　　My boy, he went to sea, long and long ago,
　　Curls of brown were slipping underneath his cap,
　　He looked at me from blue and steely eyes;
　　Natty, straight and true, he stepped away,
　　My boy, he went to sea.
All day long in fog and wind,
The waves have flung their beating crests
Against the palisades of adamant.

WAITING

Today I will let the old boat stand
Where the sweep of the harbor tide comes in
To the pulse of a far, deep-steady sway.
And I will rest and dream and sit on the deck
    Watching the world go by
And take my pay for many hard days gone I
    remember.

I will choose what clouds I like
In the great white fleets that wander the blue
As I lie on my back or loaf at the rail.
And I will listen as the veering winds kiss me and
    fold me
And put on my brow the touch of the world's great
    will.

Daybreak will hear the heart of the boat beat,
    Engine throb and piston play
In the quiver and leap at call of life.
Tomorrow we move in the gaps and heights
On changing floors of unlevel seas
And no man shall stop us and no man follow
For ours is the quest of an unknown shore
And we are husky and lusty and shouting-gay.

FROM THE SHORE

A lone gray bird,
Dim-dipping, far-flying,
Alone in the shadows and grandeurs and tumults
Of night and the sea
And the stars and storms.

Out over the darkness it wavers and hovers,
Out into the gloom it swings and batters,
Out into the wind and the rain and the vast,
Out into the pit of a great black world,
Where fogs are at battle, sky-driven, sea-blown,
Love of mist and rapture of flight,
Glories of chance and hazards of death
On its eager and palpitant wings.

Out into the deep of the great dark world,
Beyond the long borders where foam and drift
Of the sundering waves are lost and gone
On the tides that plunge and rear and crumble.

UPLANDS IN MAY

Wonder as of old things
Fresh and fair come back
Hangs over pasture and road.
Lush in the lowland grasses rise
And upland beckons to upland.
The great strong hills are humble.

DREAM GIRL

You will come one day in a waver of love,
Tender as dew, impetuous as rain,
The tan of the sun will be on your skin,
The purr of the breeze in your murmuring speech,
You will pose with a hill-flower grace.

You will come, with your slim, expressive arms,
A poise of the head no sculptor has caught
And nuances spoken with shoulder and neck,
Your face in a pass-and-repass of moods
As many as skies in delicate change
Of cloud and blue and flimmering sun.

Yet,
You may not come, O girl of a dream,
We may but pass as the world goes by
And take from a look of eyes into eyes,
A film of hope and a memoried day.

PLOWBOY

After the last red sunset glimmer,
Black on the line of a low hill rise,
Formed into moving shadows, I saw
A plowboy and two horses lined against the
    gray,
Plowing in the dusk the last furrow.
The turf had a gleam of brown,
And smell of soil was in the air,
And, cool and moist, a haze of April.

I shall remember you long,
Plowboy and horses against the sky in shadow.
I shall remember you and the picture
You made for me,
Turning the turf in the dusk
And haze of an April gloaming.

BROADWAY

I shall never forget you, Broadway
Your golden and calling lights.

I'll remember you long,
Tall-walled river of rush and play.

Hearts that know you hate you
And lips that have given you laughter
Have gone to their ashes of life and its roses,
Cursing the dreams that were lost
In the dust of your harsh and trampled stones.

OLD WOMAN

The owl-car clatters along, dogged by the echo
From building and battered paving-stone;
The headlight scoffs at the mist
And fixes its yellow rays in the cold slow rain;
Against a pane I press my forehead
And drowsily look on the walls and sidewalks.

The headlight finds the way
And life is gone from the wet and the welter—
Only an old woman, bloated, disheveled and bleared.
Far-wandered waif of other days,
Huddles for sleep in a doorway,
Homeless.

NOON HOUR

She sits in the dust at the walls
　　And makes cigars,
Bending at the bench
With fingers wage-anxious,
Changing her sweat for the day's pay.

Now the noon hour has come,
And she leans with her bare arms
On the windowsill over the river,
Leans and feels at her throat
Cool-moving things out of the free open ways:

At her throat and eyes and nostrils
The touch and the blowing cool
Of great free ways beyond the walls.

'BOES

I waited today for a freight train to pass.

Cattle cars with steers butting their horns against the bars, went by.

And a half a dozen hoboes stood on bumpers between cars.

Well, the cattle are respectable, I thought.

Every steer has its transportation paid for by the farmer sending it to market,

While the hoboes are lawbreakers in riding a railroad train without a ticket.

It reminded me of ten days I spent in the Allegheny County jail in Pittsburgh.

I got ten days even though I was a veteran of the Spanish-American war.

Cooped in the same cell with me was an old man, a bricklayer and a booze-fighter.

But it just happened he, too, was a veteran soldier, and he had fought to preserve the Union and free the niggers.

We were three in all, the other being a Lithuanian who got drunk on pay day at the steel works and got to fighting a policeman;

All the clothes he had was a shirt, pants and shoes— somebody got his hat and coat and what money he had left over when he got drunk.

UNDER A TELEPHONE POLE

I am a copper wire slung in the air,
Slim against the sun I make not even a clear line of
 shadow.
Night and day I keep singing—humming and thrum-
 ming:
It is love and war and money; it is the fighting and the
 tears, the work and want,
Death and laughter of men and women passing through
 me, carrier of your speech,
In the rain and the wet dripping, in the dawn and the
 shine drying,
     A copper wire.

I AM THE PEOPLE, THE MOB

I am the people—the mob—the crowd—the mass.
Do you know that all the great work of the world is done
    through me?
I am the workingman, the inventor, the maker of the
    world's food and clothes.
I am the audience that witnesses history. The Napoleons
    come from me and the Lincolns. They die. And then
    I send forth more Napoleons and Lincolns.
I am the seed ground. I am a prairie that will stand for
    much plowing. Terrible storms pass over me. I for-
    get. The best of me is sucked out and wasted. I
    forget. Everything but Death comes to me and
    makes me work and give up what I have. And I
    forget.
Sometimes I growl, shake myself and spatter a few red
    drops for history to remember. Then—I forget.
When I, the People, learn to remember, when I, the
    People, use the lessons of yesterday and no longer
    forget who robbed me last year, who played me for
    a fool—then there will be no speaker in all the world
    say the name: "The People," with any fleck of a
    sneer in his voice or any far-off smile of derision.
The mob—the crowd—the mass—will arrive then.

GOVERNMENT

The Government—I heard about the Government and I
went out to find it. I said I would look closely at it
when I saw it.
Then I saw a policeman dragging a drunken man to the
callaboose. It was the Government in action.
I saw a ward alderman slip into an office one morning
and talk with a judge. Later in the day the judge
dismissed a case against a pickpocket who was a live
ward worker for the alderman. Again I saw this was
the Government, doing things.
I saw militiamen level their rifles at a crowd of workingmen who were trying to get other workingmen to
stay away from a shop where there was a strike on.
Government in action.

Everywhere I saw that Government is a thing made of
men, that Government has blood and bones, it is
many mouths whispering into many ears, sending
telegrams, aiming rifles, writing orders, saying "yes"
and "no."

Government dies as the men who form it die and are laid
away in their graves and the new Government that
comes after is human, made of heartbeats of blood,
ambitions, lusts, and money running through it all,
money paid and money taken, and money covered
up and spoken of with hushed voices.
A Government is just as secret and mysterious and sensi-
tive as any human sinner carrying a load of germs,
traditions and corpuscles handed down from fathers
and mothers away back.

LANGUAGES

There are no handles upon a language
Whereby men take hold of it
And mark it with signs for its remembrance.
It is a river, this language,
Once in a thousand years
Breaking a new course
Changing its way to the ocean.
It is mountain effluvia
Moving to valleys
And from nation to nation
Crossing borders and mixing.
Languages die like rivers.
Words wrapped round your tongue today
And broken to shape of thought
Between your teeth and lips speaking
Now and today
Shall be faded hieroglyphics
Ten thousand years from now.
Sing—and singing—remember
Your song dies and changes
And is not here tomorrow
Any more than the wind
Blowing ten thousand years ago.

LETTERS TO DEAD IMAGISTS

EMILY DICKINSON:
You gave us the bumble bee who has a soul,
The everlasting traveler among the hollyhocks,
And how God plays around a backyard garden.

STEVIE CRANE:
War is kind and we never knew the kindness of war till
    you came;
Nor the black riders and clashes of spear and shield out
    of the sea,
Nor the mumblings and shots that rise from dreams on
    call.

SHEEP

Thousands of sheep, soft-footed, black-nosed sheep—one by one going up the hill and over the fence—one by one four-footed pattering up and over—one by one wiggling their stub tails as they take the short jump and go over—one by one silently unless for the multitudinous drumming of their hoofs as they move on and go over—thousands and thousands of them in the gray haze of evening just after sundown—one by one slanting in a long line to pass over the hill—

I am the slow, long-legged Sleepyman and I love you sheep in Persia, California, Argentine, Australia, or Spain—you are the thoughts that help me when I, the Sleepyman, lay my hands on the eyelids of the children of the world at eight o'clock every night—you thousands and thousands of sheep in a procession of dusk making an endless multitudinous drumming on the hills with your hoofs.

THE RED SON

I love your faces I saw the many years
I drank your milk and filled my mouth
With your home talk, slept in your house
And was one of you.
                    But a fire burns in my heart.
Under the ribs where pulses thud
And flitting between bones of skull
Is the push, the endless mysterious command,
                    Saying:
"I leave you behind—
You for the little hills and the years all alike,
You with your patient cows and old houses
Protected from the rain,
I am going away and I never come back to you;
Crags and high rough places call me,
Great places of death
Where men go empty-handed
And pass over smiling
To the star-drift on the horizon rim.
My last whisper shall be alone, unknown;
I shall go to the city and fight against it,
And make it give me passwords
Of luck and love, women worth dying for,
And money.
                    I go where you wist not of
                    Nor I nor any man nor woman.
                    I only know I go to storms
                    Grappling against things wet and naked."
There is no pity of it and no blame.
None of us is in the wrong.
After all it is only this:
                    You for the little hills and I go away.

THE MIST

I am the mist, the impalpable mist,
Back of the thing you seek.
My arms are long,
Long as the reach of time and space.

Some toil and toil, believing,
Looking now and again on my face,
Catching a vital, olden glory.

But no one passes me,
I tangle and snare them all.
I am the cause of the Sphinx,
The voiceless, baffled, patient Sphinx.

I was at the first of things,
I will be at the last.
    I am the primal mist
    And no man passes me;
    My long impalpable arms
    Bar them all.

THE JUNK MAN

I am glad God saw Death
And gave Death a job taking care of all who are tired of
    living:

When all the wheels in a clock are worn and slow and the
    connections loose
And the clock goes on ticking and telling the wrong time
    from hour to hour
And people around the house joke about what a bum
    clock it is,
How glad the clock is when the big Junk Man drives his
    wagon
Up to the house and puts his arms around the clock and
    says:
        "You don't belong here,
        You gotta come
        Along with me,"
How glad the clock is then, when it feels the arms of the
    Junk Man close around it and carry it away.

SILVER NAILS

A man was crucified. He came to the city a stranger, was accused, and nailed to a cross. He lingered hanging. Laughed at the crowd. "The nails are iron," he said, "You are cheap. In my country when we crucify we use silver nails . . ." So he went jeering. They did not understand him at first. Later they talked about him in changed voices in the saloons, bowling alleys, and churches. It came over them every man is crucified only once in his life and the law of humanity dictates silver nails be used for the job. A statue was erected to him in a public square. Not having gathered his name when he was among them, they wrote him as John Silvernail on the statue.

GYPSY

I asked a gypsy pal
To imitate an old image
And speak old wisdom.
She drew in her chin,
Made her neck and head
The top piece of a Nile obelisk
    and said:
Snatch off the gag from thy mouth, child,
And be free to keep silence.
Tell no man anything for no man listens,
Yet hold thy lips ready to speak.

In Reckless
Ecstasy

AND A MAN'S A FOOL

And a man's a fool if things there are
That seethe and clash in his ardent brain?
And the ache to utter and to see in word
The silhouette of a brooding soul
Is the childish play of a childish man?
To poetize!—this is the butt and the target's eye
For the by-word, fling and gibe.

Pass on! all ye who do
From the core of your souls
And the heart of your hearts.
Pass on! all ye whose voices sound
With a throb for all and a throe for each.
Like giants stride you thru the crowd,
Your hands touch theirs as kin,
But in the cool and calm,
O'er the press and stir
Of the multitudes,
Your eyes, your eyes, your eager eyes!

TO WHOM MY HAND
GOES OUT

The unapplauded ones who bear
  No badges on their breasts,
Who pass us on the street, with calm,
  Unfearing, patient eyes,
Like dumb cart-horses in the sleet!

The unperturbed who feel the oldness—
  All the sadness of the world—
Yet somehow feel the sacredness
  Of grime upon the hands,
And even know the rush of pity
  For the ones who know not
That some Power builds a callus out of blisters.

  The eyes! the eyes that pierce
The dust and smoke of unrewarded toil
  And count it gain and joy
To have lived and sweat and wrought
  And been a man!

THE DEAD-SEA APPLE

Had it been beauty past my reach,
　　Or far beyond my humble ken,
There would have been a tint of joy
　　In all the pain of longing then.

But that the red, sweet hues should fade
　　Into a dust, and nameless ash,
And promises to gray-sick rot—
　　O God, that sight and sense thus clash!

A HOMELY WINTER IDYL

Great, long, lean clouds in sullen host
   Along the skyline passed today;
While overhead I've only seen
   A leaden sky the whole long day.

My heart would gloomily have mused
   Had I not seen those queer, old crows
Stop short in their mad frolicking
   And pose for me in long, black rows.

17

Polymer–Clay Nanocomposites: Synthesis and Properties

SYED QUTUBUDDIN and XIAOAN FU
Case Western Reserve University, Cleveland, Ohio

I. INTRODUCTION

Conventional polymer composites are widely used in diverse applications, such as construction, transportation, electronics, and consumer products. Composites offer improved properties, including higher strength and stiffness, compared to pristine polymers. The properties of polymer composites are greatly affected by the dimension and microstructure of the dispersed phase. Nanocomposites are a new class of composites that have a dispersed phase with at least one ultrafine dimension, typically a few nanometers [1–3]. Nanocomposites possess special properties not shared by conventional composites, due primarily to large interfacial area per unit volume or weight of the dispersed phase (e.g., 750 m^2/g). Clay layers dispersed at the nanoscale in a polymer matrix act as a reinforcing phase to form polymer–clay nanocomposites, an important class of organic–inorganic nanocomposites. These nanocomposites are also referred to as polymer–silicate nanocomposites and organic–inorganic hybrids. Polymer–clay nanocomposites can drastically improve mechanical reinforcement and high-temperature durability, provide enhanced barrier properties, and reduce flammability [4–6]. Clays that have a high aspect ratio of silicate nanolayers are desirable for polymer reinforcement.

Colloid and surface chemistry play important roles in the synthesis of polymer–clay nanocomposites. Dispersion of clay layers in polymers is hindered by the inherent tendency to form face-to-face stacks in agglomerated tactoids due to high interlayer cohesive energy. Nanoscale dispersion of the clay tactoids into individual nanolayers is known as exfoliation or delamination. Exfoliation is further prevented by the incompatibility between hydrophilic clay and hydrophobic polymers. Treatment or functionalization of clay by adsorption of organic molecules weakens the interlayer cohesive energy. Intercalation, i.e., penetration of organic molecules into the clay interlayers, increases the compatibility between clay and polymer matrix. Due to the negative charge on the clay surface, cationic surfactants and polymers are commonly used for intercalation. The ion exchange of inorganic cations in clay galleries by organic cations renders the clay organophilic. Such organoclays have found large-scale applications for decades in cosmetics, drilling mud, paints, coatings, inks, and wastewater treatment [7]. There is a growing interest in the surface chemistry of clays in pursuit of nanocomposite synthesis using specific monomers, prepolymers, and polymer melts. This chapter provides a review of recent developments in the synthesis and properties of modified clay and polymer–clay nanocomposites.

II. CLAY STRUCTURE AND DISPERSION IN POLYMER

Clay consists of small crystalline particles made up of aluminosilicates of various compositions, with possible iron and magnesium substitutions by alkalis and alkaline earth elements [8–12]. The basic silicon-oxygen unit is a tetrahedron, with four oxygen atoms surrounding the central silicon. The tetrahedra are linked to form hexagonal rings. This pattern repeats in two dimensions to form a sheet. Aluminum, in combination with oxygen, forms an octahedron, with the aluminum at the center, and the octahedra link to form a more closely packed two-dimensional sheet. There are two basic types of clay structures (1:1 and 2:1). Kaolinite is 1:1 type of nonswelling dioctahedral clay. The kaolinite crystal is a sheet of alumina octahedra sitting on top of a sheet of silica tetrahedra. The apical oxygen atoms from the silica are shared with the aluminum atoms of the upper layer. The other basic type of clay is of the 2:1 type (i.e., two sheets of silica to one of alumina or two sheets of silica to one of magnesium oxide). The two parent materials are pyrophyllite and talc, with alumina and magnesia, respectively, in the central layer.

Clays used in preparing polymer–clay nanocomposites belong to the 2:1 layered structure type. A member of the 2:1 family, montmorillonite is one of the most interesting and widely investigated clays for polymer nanocomposites. The structure of montmorillonite consists of layers made up of one octahedral alumina sheet sandwiched between two tetrahedral silica sheets, as shown in Figure 1 [8]. Stacking of the silicate layers leads to a regular van der Waals gap between the layers. Approximately one in six of the aluminum ions in the octahedral layers of montmorillonite is isomorphously substituted by magne-

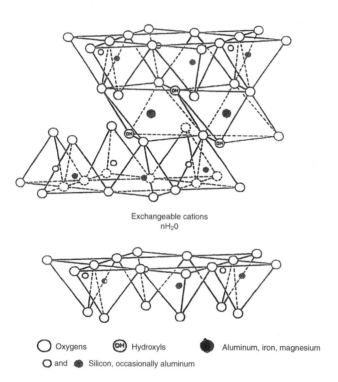

Exchangeable cations
nH_2O

○ Oxygens   ⊙ Hydroxyls   ● Aluminum, iron, magnesium
○ and ◐ Silicon, occasionally aluminum

FIG. 1   Idealized structure of a montmorillonite layer showing two tetrahedral-site sheets fused to an octahedral-site sheet (2:1 type). (From Ref. 8.)

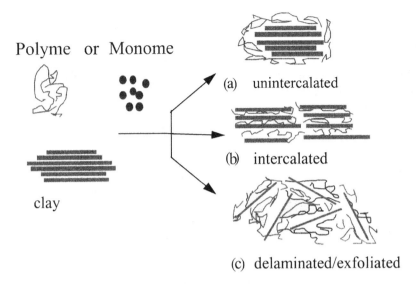

Polyme or Monome

clay

(a) unintercalated

(b) intercalated

(c) delaminated/exfoliated

FIG. 2 Schematic illustration of three types of polymer–clay composites.

sium or other divalent ions. The isomorphic substitution renders negative charges that are counterbalanced by cations residing in the interlayer. Pristine clay usually contains hydrated inorganic cations such as Na^+, K^+, and Ca^{2+}. When the inorganic cations are exchanged by organic cations, such as from surfactants and polyelectrolytes, the clay surface changes from hydrophilic to hydrophobic or organophilic [13,14]. The organic cations lower the surface energy and decrease the cohesive energy by expanding the interlayer distance, thus facilitating the wetting and intercalation of monomer or polymer. In addition, the organic cations may contain various functional groups that react with monomer or polymer resin to improve interfacial adhesion between clay nanolayers and polymer matrix.

Complete dispersion or exfoliation of clay tactoids in a monomer or polymer matrix may involve three steps similar to the dispersion of powders in liquids, as identified by Parfitt [15]. The first step is wetting the surface of clay tactoids by monomer or polymer molecules. The second step is intercalation or infiltration of the monomer or polymer into the clay galleries, and the third step is exfoliation of clay layers. The first and second steps are determined by thermodynamics, while the third step is controlled by mechanical and reaction driving forces. The dispersion of clay tactoids in a polymer matrix can result in the formation of three types of composites, as shown in Figure 2. The first type is a conventional composite that contains clay tactoids with the nanolayers aggregated in un-intercalated face-to-face form. In this case, the clay tactoids are dispersed simply as a segregated phase, resulting in poor mechanical properties of the composite. The second type is intercalated polymer–clay nanocomposite, which is formed by the infiltration of one or more molecular layers of polymer into the clay host galleries. The last type is exfoliated polymer–clay nanocomposites, characterized by a low clay content, a monolithic structure, and a separation between clay layers that depends on the polymer content of the composite. Exfoliation is particularly desirable for improving specific properties that are affected by the degree of dispersion and resulting interfacial area between polymer and clay nanolayers.

Homogeneous dispersion of clay nanolayers in a polymer matrix provides maximum reinforcement via distribution of stress and deflection of cracks resulting from an applied load. Interactions between exfoliated nanolayers with large interfacial area and surrounding polymer matrix lead to higher tensile strength, modulus, and thermal stability [4–6]. Conventional polymer–filler composites containing micron-size aggregated tactoids also improve stiffness, but at the expense of strength, elongation, and toughness. However, exfoliated clay nanocomposites of Nylon-6 and epoxy have shown improvements in all aspects of thermomechanical behavior. Exfoliation of silicate nanolayers with high aspect ratio also provides other performance enhancements that are not achievable with conventional particulate composites. The impermeable clay nanolayers provide a tortuous pathway for a permeant to diffuse through the nanocomposite. The hindered diffusion in nanocomposites leads to enhanced barrier property, reduced swelling by solvent, and improvements in chemical stability and flame retardance.

III. CATION EXCHANGE OF CLAY WITH SURFACTANTS

Industrial applications of organoclays [7,16] have stimulated scientific efforts to understand the mechanism of surfactant ion exchange and adsorption. The adsorption of cationic surfactants onto a homoionic montmorillonite dispersed in water was found to be independent of the size of hydrophilic head group of cationic surfactants at its natural pH [17]. The amount of cationic surfactant adsorbed as a monolayer is almost the same as the cationic exchange capacity, CEC. The critical coagulation concentrations are also close to CEC. The completeness of the exchange of inorganic cations by cationic surfactants and the chemical adsorption stability of surfactant–clay complexes greatly affect the application of organoclays [18,19]. The structure of the adsorption layer of cationic surfactants in the galleries of swelling clays depends strongly on the initial degree of clay dispersion. Initial conditions that correspond to a homogeneous dispersion of swelling clay (e.g., Na-saturated clay and low ionic strength) result in random organic/inorganic cation distribution in the interlayers. Also, the adsorbed surfactant layer has a loose structure at low organic cation concentration.

Adsorption isotherms and precise calorimetric experiments were used to identify different types of adsorption and quantify the interactions between cationic surfactants and clay [20,21]. The type of clay and the alkyl chain length of surfactant significantly affect the amount and the enthalpy of adsorption, which is exothermic. Several models have been proposed to account for surfactant adsorption on solid surfaces. However, these models rely on assumptions about the structure of the adsorbed surfactant layer [22–24]. Bohmer and Koopal [25,26] investigated surfactant adsorption on nonswelling clay surfaces using a self-consistent lattice model. The model predicts the structure of the adsorbed layers and a gradual increase in surfactant adsorption with surfactant concentration. Most experimental data supporting the foregoing models were obtained with nonswelling solids. Swelling layered clays certainly exhibit some differences in adsorption behavior, because the structure of the adsorbed surfactant is quite different from that on nonswelling clays. The intercalation of surfactant in swelling clays is discussed in the next section.

IV. INTERCALATION OF CATIONIC SURFACTANTS IN CLAY GALLERIES

The exchange of inorganic cations by organic surfactant ions in the clay galleries not only makes the organoclay surface compatible with monomer or polymer matrix, but also de-